Please Pray with Me
Prayers for People at Worship

Earle W. Fike, Jr.

Foreword
by
Leonard Sweet

BRETHREN PRESS
Elgin, Illinois

Please Pray with Me
Prayers for People at Worship
Earle W. Fike, Jr.

BRETHREN PRESS, 1451 Dundee Avenue, Elgin, IL 60120

Biblical quotations, unless otherwise noted, are from the
Revised Standard Version of the Bible, copyrighted 1946,
1952, and 1971 by the Division of Christian Education,
National Council of Churches, and are used by permission.

Cover design by David Vandelinder

Manufactured in the United States of America

FOREWORD

HAVE you ever walked into a room where people were praying? Then you have sensed that hallowed aura, that special power that the earth exhales into the atmosphere of prayer-inhaling places. *Please Pray with Me* has the body of a book of prayers. But it has the mind of a theologian (which Evagrius of Pontus defined in the fourth century as "one whose prayer is true"), and the spirit of a room filled with praying people.

Until now I have never been even a remote fan of collections of prayers. For one thing, too many prayers push against an open door. When people open their mouths to pray they immediately begin talking out of a different dictionary, and with a distinct diction, forcing their mouths to form unnatural accents and airs. This makes praying a struggle for both the participant and the recipient, both of whom inevitably fail to relax in each other's company. Anyone who doubts the credence of Jung's conviction that "religion is a defense against the experience of God" need only turn pages heaving with these pious heavy-breathings or step into room squally with such windy formations.

Second, praying should open doors rather than close them. Published prayers master the ventriloquist's trick of putting words into someone else's mouth, words which come out sounding amazingly like a Sunday homily or soapbox punditry—with large amounts of Sunday school cliches and Sunday supplement advertisements thrown in for our good measure and God's pleasure. A preacherly tone is tolerable in sermons, barely. A stuffily affected and reverent air in which spiritual swoonings and swoopings leap smugly about is insufferable.

What distinguishes this book from the ruck of door shuttings? Instead of words chasing away prayer, when reading Earle Fike's prayers I literally could not keep myself from praying. *Please Pray with Me* is a cathedral gallery of swing-doors, each escalating to higher spheres of reality and influence where the boundaries between the spiritual and the material are thin and permeable. At one moment we enter the half-open doors of Heaven. The next moment we escape the clanging gates of Hell. Whichever, Earle Fike ushers us into the presence of the Almighty with the spirit of a fellow traveler. He does not pray off the sweat of other people's brows. He risks dangerous liaisons with life, and with God.

This means we, the readers, are about to enter into an unusually intimate relationship with the author. By speaking with almost poetic energy about the anxiety-producing, gratitude-evoking, eternity-gesturing experiences of life, we are given memorable metaphors that have the power of metamorphosis. Fike knows that metaphors are the very stuff of which life is made; that images possess a generative and curative power. These prayers helped me to will, to will, God's will. Not too hard, not too soft, but just right: they continue to work their way in my life, making me a better "housekeeper of the heart."

Every prayer in this book is a personalized recital of compelling urgency and lingering appeal. In other words, the fundamental musicality of praying is never really hidden but is indeed bidden through Fike's frequent structuring of prayer—ACTS (Adoration, Confession, Thanksgiving, Supplication) around familiar hymns. To be sure, these prayers are not always an easy tune to sing. But even when Fike hears the screak of some dark angel invading our tranquility and demanding to be reckoned with, our fears are drowned out and lost in the chorus of grace. In short, the Christian life comes to resemble the ululating advance of lapping waves up a beach, a motion of blend and balance between petition and praise, personal and communal, silence and speech, joy and brokenness, "Thumb screwing and hand shaking," luminous heights and cavernous depths.

During dry spells of the spirit, dark nights of the soul, valleys of the shadow, descending fogs of disbelief, even joys unspeakable and full of glory, what will be our constant prop and comfort? What phrases will stumble off our lips? My guess is that for most of us it will not be neo-orthodox dogmatics, or post-modern deconstructionism or narrative theology story-tellings. Rather, it will be praying-by-numbers psalmody or poop-sheet prayers that sing . . . prayers like the ones you are about to find here in *Please Pray with Me.*

Leonard I. Sweet, President
United Theological Seminary
Dayton, Ohio

INTRODUCTION

P RAYING with the congregation during Sunday morning worship is a privilege. It should not be taken lightly. Those of us who do it regularly should be open to the Spirit as we invite persons to pray with us, but that openness ought never to mean a last minute impromptu eruption of words and thoughts shared in the crisis of needing to say something at the point in the order of worship which calls for "The Pastoral Prayer." It takes careful thought and preparation to make the pastoral prayer a significant experience.

Public praying with the congregation ought to be an invitation for the listener to participate. The purpose is to invite assent; to say things which people might not themselves think to say but which, when it is said, such a kinship is felt that there is a silent "yes!" The purpose is to lift before God expressions and feelings which enable those praying along to say, "that's me; that's the way I feel; that's what I would like to say to God."

If the prayer takes things seriously but is non-judgmental; if it shows straightforward honesty yet is compassionate, a by-product of this kind of corporate "assent" is that the people praying with the pastor develop a trust for the way the pastor understands. The quality of pastoral care is enriched.

Most of the prayers in this collection were actually prayed with the Stone Church of the Brethren in Huntingdon, Pennsylvania.[1] They are accustomed to hearing me say, "Please Pray With Me." The prayers were all written ahead of time, so as to be concentrated rather than rambling. Conserving time and words invites attention. And while the written form is used during the prayer, the prayers are prayed rather than read.

When preparing prayers to be prayed with the congregation, I strive for images, descriptions, analogies, and illusions which have emotion and power along with a heavy dash of "everydayness" to provide freshness! I also try to think about specific persons in the congregation and events which influence the lives of all of us. But I work at generalizing the specifics so as to invite persons into real situations without revealing too much or raising unnecessary questions about "who or what the pastor is referring to."

The prayers are set in the context of any given Sunday morning order of worship. They are often prepared in relation to some theme or some immediate worship event. Sometimes they are in response to the scripture, sometimes in response to the morning anthem, sometimes in response to a hymn. You will therefore recognize some word usage related to language from hymns, anthems, and scripture.

Special thanks needs to be expressed to Judy Cooper, Administrative Secretary at Stone Church, for her assistance in preparing the manuscript, and to Esther Doyle, chief encourager and "arm twister" for this project. Also, much appreciation to the good people at Stone Church who are making my tenure with them a joy and a privilege. They are a supportive and nurturing garden in which to plant corporate prayers with God. They comment about the prayers and ask for copies, and hence, by their encouragement, these prayers with them are now prayers with you. Please pray with me!

Earle W. Fike, Jr.
Huntingdon, Pennsylvania
January 4, 1988

1. Some dozen of these prayers were prayed with the Elizabethtown Church of the Brethren, Elizabethtown, Pennsylvania during a nine year tenure with them.

O WORD, which was in the beginning, be with us in the beginning of this New Year. By virtue of the media, we can review 365 days in 60 seconds, and while the experience is interesting, it is hardly gratifying. We see the violence which characterizes us; the injustice which plagues us; the insatiable hunger for power which controls us, yet gives us no peace. And 365 days in 60 seconds only reminds us the more of how life seems to be hurrying past without our full participation. We have much to learn in this New Year which we have not yet absorbed. We have much to do we have not really tried. O Word, which was in the beginning, in this new year, lead us in your righteousness.

O Word, which is still with us, teach us how to participate in the fullness of life. We long to learn how to walk the fine line between justice and celebration; between genuine care for others and joy of living; between petition and praise. We are so conscious of all that is happening which should concern us that we almost feel guilty when we feel good. We do not desire to ignore the critical and pressing issues of the year, but Oh!, how we long to be able to rejoice freely in that which is a blessing. How we long to give ourselves to pure joy without some shadow shading our pleasure. O Word, which was in the beginning, be with us in the days of this new year. Lead us in your righteousness, that we may be both responsible and joyful.

O Word, which is light to our way, and comfort to our pain, be with all who review last year with a sense of loss, with grief, with pain, with uncertainty, with anger at interruption or brokenness. Give them hope for better days.

O Word, which is our beginning and ending, gather our lives in your hand. Inspire us to what we can become; energize us for the things our lives can contribute; strengthen us against the storms which may beset us; and enable us to live the days of this new year in such a way that when they come to their end, we may with right good confidence say, "Word which was in the beginning, it was good to be with you and your people and our loved ones for another year." Through Christ we pray, AMEN.

O GOD of all that there is and God of each one of us; God of the vast expanse of the universe and of any private minute claimed by any one of us; hear our prayer.

Create in us a clean heart, O God. When life wearies in sameness; when we're busy yet there seems so little meaning in what we do; when wrong choice or injustice from another leaves a residue of leftover pain, hurt, or anger which preoccupies our time; in all such times, O Lord, how we long for a clean heart and a right spirit. You alone have the eraser which gives us fresh new beginnings, Lord. We may apologize; we may feel sorry; but you are the one who forgives and helps us to forgive. We must ask for it. We have to want new beginnings. In our better moments we do. Create in us a clean heart, O God.

Each one of us has persons we love and care about; family, friends, neighbors. Each of us has persons for whom we are concerned. Some face severe illness; some are hemmed in by financial despair; some have trouble making wise decisions; some have trouble learning from past history; some get up to pain every day; some are withered by hostility and broken by old hurts. In these moments of quiet, hear our prayer for them. Create for each of them, clean hearts and a renewed right spirit within them.

A cluttered heart has trouble recognizing joy, O God. A frantic heart has little time to revel in the goodness of the simple love of friends or family. A weary heart sees more grey than color; hears more noise than music; drags off to work rather than labors in a vocation. A blinded heart misses the smile of someone who cares; the beauty of a winter sunset; the geometric dazzle of a single snowflake. O God, create in us clean hearts, that we may rejoice in the goodness of life.

While a clean heart may not change our circumstances, it can at least renew our perspective. In the gift of a clean heart, O God, you give us strength to change the things which can be changed; courage to accept the things which we cannot change; and the grace and wisdom to know the difference. Thank you. AMEN

3 THIRD PRAYER IN JANUARY

O CHRIST, true light, behold the kinds of darkness which threaten and frighten us. There is the distant, yet near, darkness of war and hatred between persons. Forgive us for seeming to have only one solution to national differences. Teach us the things of peace. And accept our thanks for every wise and possible effort being made for peace; in the Middle East; in developing countries; in nations, large and small; and in Central America. O Christ, our true light, triumph over all the shades of national and international night.

There has been, this week in our community, the darkness of a young man's suicide. We pray for him, that in your mercy, you might receive him and help him. We pray for all who felt close to him. Give them wisdom to distinguish between wishing they could have known how to help, and feeling bad because they did not do something. Save them from false guilt, for none of us causes another to take his or her life. We pray for us all, that we might keep tuned and sensitive to those who feel as if life is more thumb screwing than hand shaking; more despair then joy. Even in the midst of darkness, we desire to be your caring people. O Christ, our true light, triumph over all the shades of neighborly night which plague us.

There are always, O God, the shadows of personal pain, brokenness, or sickness which darken the lives of friends and family and neighbor. We remember now those who need our prayers for healing and strength and hope. In this moment of silence, hear our private prayers. O Christ, our true light, triumph over all the shades of night which settle on those near and dear to us.

O Christ, our true light, in the midst of darkness, teach us how to rejoice in the light. If our cup runs over, give us grace to say so with joy. If our life has meaning, give us grace to say so with thanksgiving. If there are those who care about us and love us and encourage us to become what we can be, give us grace to receive and relish that support; and give it back, full measure, in return.

O Christ, our true light, we feel so inadequate in prayer. Gather all that is difficult for us to admit or say, and complete our prayers as we pray as you taught us to pray, OUR FATHER, WHO ART IN HEAVEN . . .

4 FOURTH PRAYER IN JANUARY

O UR PRAYER today is in the form of a bidding prayer. Please pray with me, in your own way. You may follow the suggestions if they are helpful to you.

Begin by thinking of a name you wish to use in addressing God.

Now think of one way in which you were blessed this past week. Call God by name and thank God for the blessing.

Think of a family member who has been most on your mind in the last days. Pray for that person by name and need.

Think of this bright day; the winter thaw; the heat of the sun on your face as you look up; the promise of spring. Thank God for it.

Think of some friend or neighbor for whom life is particularly difficult right now. Pray for that person by name.

Think of some world issue which easily upsets you. Ask God to help all people of the world and to help you to know how you can help.

Think of someone whom you have trouble liking; someone with whom you have a history of problems. Pray for that person by name. And pray for yourself, that you may find help in dealing with your own feelings.

Think of someone hurting from lost relationships or loneliness. Pray for that person by name.

Think of someone hurting from disease; perhaps real pain or the pain of not knowing what's coming in the days ahead. Pray for that person by name.

Think of our church, its life and ministry. Ask God to help us see what we ought to be doing, and then help us do what we ought to do.

Think of yourself. What demon will not let you go? What one thing would you like to have changed in your life? Ask God to help you.

Think of the difference between hostility and peace. Ask God to strengthen and bring to fruition all hope you have for peace.

"Immortal and Invisible God," so far yet so near, thank you for hearing the prayers we have prayed in Jesus' name. AMEN.

5 FIFTH PRAYER IN JANUARY

GREAT is Thy Faithfulness, O God. We have ignored you; forgotten you; placed other things before you; made you a sometime priority. We have accused you; abused you; spoken all manner of descriptions against you. We have called to you; pled with you; bargained with you; and through it all you have not turned away. You have not left us to ourselves. You have been our God when we have not been your people. Great is your faithfulness to us, O God.

We have made war when you call us to peace. We have hated when you call us to love. We have judged the speck in our brother's and sister's eye while peering through a two by four in our own. We have chosen violence when you call us to servanthood. We have put our trust in strength when you speak to us of weakness. With it all, you have not given up on us. You stay with us with a tenacity that at once puts us to shame and blesses us. Great is your faithfulness to us, O God.

"Morning by morning, new mercies we see." In the midst of rejection or abuse, love will rear its head in a caring of some friend. In the midst of problems that tie us in knots, the deft fingers of important values unravel the bind and free us to live with meaning. Despair is fractured by some bright ray of hope; life's sameness is shattered by some new melody. Great is your faithfulness to us, O God.

When we are sick, you give us persons who can relieve anxiety and point us to some path toward health. Great is your faithfulness through physicians, nurses, and health care professionals. When we are lonely you give us a community of faith for support. Great is your faithfulness through your church. When we are faced with the terminal, you put before us the bright colors of the eternal. Great is your faithfulness in the technicolor rainbow of your mercy and love. When we are weak, you put your arms under us and around us in strength. Great is your faithfulness in the comfort and courage of your Holy Spirit. When we don't know what to do with ourselves, you point us to open paths of service. Great is your faithfulness in keeping before us, your world and our neighbor.

"All we have needed your hand has provided." Thank you, God, for your great faithfulness. AMEN

O GOD, we thank you that you treat us as if all were one; and each one as if there were only one. We thank you that we are all held together in your love; and that none of us gets lost in the crowd. We thank you that you hear our prayers; the prayers we feel awkward about; the prayers we are hesitant to pray; and the prayers we feel that we do not know the right words to pray. We thank you that you know us well enough to hear our thoughts, our yearnings, our stumblings, our grumblings, our secret hopes, even when we dare not; even when we cannot put them into words. We thank you that anytime we turn toward you, the arms of your grace and love are there to enfold us. We thank you that the truth of that love and grace cannot be bought or earned or bargained for. Since it is a gift which you give and which we can only receive, give us wisdom to joyfully receive it.

Life is such a fearful and wonderful thing, Lord. We did not ask to have it, but having it, we wish it to be full of joy and meaning. Jesus grant us this: the ability to as easily recognize and celebrate the beautiful as we are able to itemize the ugly. Grant us the ability to as easily praise as we condemn. Grant us the ability to as easily support as we ignore. Grant us the ability to as easily express joy as we display disappointment.

Grant us some sense of worth and accomplishment which places the mark of meaning on our days. Grant us some sense of purpose, that tomorrow is something to look forward to rather than dread. Encourage us to reach outside of ourselves, and find ways to express the energy of life in benefit to the world and its people whom you so loved.

Jesus grant us this. When life tumbles in; when almost everything seems to crumble around us; when the simple things we took for granted turn into an unusual blessing; when hope frays and energy hides and a smile is something we remember we used to do; in that time, O Lord, find some special way to hold us in the palm of your hand.

Jesus grant us this. We pray for friends and loved ones with special needs; and we pray for this wonderful, unhappy, promising, stupid, gifted, fearful, mixed-up world in which we live. We have misused power and it is both an enemy and creates enemies. We have misused abundance, and what could be a blessing to almost everyone is a curse to too many. Give us and the leaders of nations the wisdom to break out of the destructive patterns of international relations, and grant us peace in our time. AMEN.

S AVIOR, like a shepherd lead us: when we don't
want to be led, lead us anyway. When we begin to
follow each other; when we begin to nibble ourselves into
precarious places; when we begin to go the easiest way;
lead us.

Savior, like a shepherd, lead us. When life seems
tainted with discouragement, lead us in the pleasant
places of real joy. When what we don't have occupies
more of our time than the blessings we have, lead us in
the green pastures of true thanksgiving. When despair
wearies our steps, rest us by leading us where the way is
easy until we regain perspective and strength.

Savior, like a shepherd lead us. How warm and
energizing are the ways of love, yet we travel roads of
bitterness and envy. How sweet is service, yet we live
with the false lolly-pop of "what's in it for me" stuck in
our mouths. Revenge, like salt water, adds to thirst rather
than quenches it, yet we choose paying back over
offering the hand of fellowship. Lead us in life's super
highway of neighborly love.

Savior, like a shepherd lead us. No shepherd can
protect sheep from all harm. We suffer physically and
emotionally. Someone loses a loved one to death; another
loses a loved one to a broken relationship. Someone
receives the bad news of a malignancy; another hears the
words, "I don't love you anymore." Someone hears the
words, "you can never get better," another hears the

words "if you were better I could love you more." O
God, for all who are bowed down in sorrow, who wish
that it would go away; who remember what life used to
be like with wistfulness and angry hurt; for all such, O
Lord, lead them like a shepherd. Hold them close until
the fear and the hurt and the pain are laid to rest.

Now, O God, we have the rest of this day, and
tomorrow we face a new day. As the days come and go
and we make our way along life's journey; savior, like a
shepherd lead us, for left to our own devices, we shall
surely choose the wrong way. But following you, we
shall wend our pilgrim way in goodness and mercy all
the days of our lives. AMEN.

O GOD, many of us do not have traditional symbols to help us begin the season of Lent. We have no Mardi Gras to celebrate, and no mark on our forehead to begin penitence. So Lent is upon us and we are hardly ready.

Lord, many of us do not look forward to Lent. None of us likes to be reminded of our shortcomings; none likes to be faced with a catalogue of mistakes. Lent seems to be a "downer," so much gloom, so many references to sin. Teach us the necessities of confession, Lord. Teach us that naming an evil is the first step to being free of it. Teach us that while grace is free, feeling contrite is necessary in order for us to receive it. Help us to learn that facing who we are is necessary in order to change and improve who we are.

O God, some of us are getting ready for spring. Some of us already have our seeds; our plans for planting. Others rejoice in every mild temperatured day, knowing other days will soon be the usual rather than the rare. Help us , O God, to translate those good and expectant feelings into our experience of Lent. For this is the season of the springtime of the soul. We plan and look with eagerness to new growth in nature. Encourage us to be as sensible about our spiritual possibilities as we are about our gardens and lawns and flowers.

Forgive us if we have seemed to be too preoccupied

with ourselves in this prayer. There are injustices which need our action. There are neighbors who need our care. There are friends who can use our demonstrations of love. Give us eyes to see and willing wills to respond; to those who need our encouragement toward health; to those who need our assurance that they are important; to those who need us to stand with them as they wait in uncertainty; to all who need our prayerful support for their wholeness.

The crocus is ready to test its new life. The geese are on their way north. A few brave buds have ventured on the limb. Make us brave toward new life, new possibilities this season, O God. For you have given, in Jesus Christ, promise rather than treats. And we desire to live with the rainbow rather than the storm. AMEN.

O GOD who so loved everyone and each one, we thank you for your inclusiveness and your specificity. In your only begotten son, there is no Greek nor Jew, no slave nor free, no male nor female. We are all equally welcome. Through him, you are equally available to everyone; and each one, by virtue of reaching out and receiving him, may have the strength and comfort of your special attention.

O God, you came not to condemn the world but to save. If we could only rid ourselves of thinking of you as some arrogant or punitive law officer hiding with divine radar to fine us for the slightest misdemeanor; and instead think of you as a loving parent, on the one hand staying our dangerous straying for our own safety, and on the other, helpfully encouraging us to grow and mature and flower into full potential. There is a wideness in your mercy like the wideness of the sea; and there is kindness in your justice which is more than liberty. But we choose to hide from you and live in fear rather than your blessed freedom.

O God, life is often puzzle and predicament for us. It is often harried and overworked. It is sometimes frightening and uncertain. In these moments we seek to borrow some extra measure of your love for persons who especially need it. In the silence of our own hearts, we mention persons who are sick and need your healing power. Now we think of persons who face serious illness

or surgery, and need special care. Now we think of
persons who are tired and frustrated, and do not know
which way to turn to relieve the pressures of life. Now
we think of persons whose family life seems to be
coming apart at the seams; who aren't sure love can be
patient and kind; who wish they themselves were more
like they would like to be treated. We remember those
who have need of food and lodging. We remember those
who are lonely and need friends. By your strength
minister to them, but do not allow us to ignore what we
ourselves can do to help in your name. You have so
loved the world. Make us ministers of your love.
Through Jesus Christ your only begotten son, AMEN.

WE STAND beneath your cross, O Christ. But we do not always glory in it. We find it difficult to comprehend; and hard to accept. The symbol is familiar, but the meaning is vague. There are truths imbedded in its design, truths about divine love, and acceptance, and forgiveness, and new life which are deeply important to us. We do not desire to ignore or forget the pain or the ugliness of the cross. But grant us, by the gift of your spirit, the ability to comprehend and rejoice in the glory of the cross.

O Christ, we see the cross itself as a despicable and inhuman form of punishment. It is so human of us to pile violence on violence as a deterrent. But from a simple logical perspective, slow torturous death does not help to balance the scales of justice. In the message of the cross is the truth that, by your power, bad things can become transformed into good things; evil can have a good side; disaster can become a form of blessing. And how we need that truth to give us comfort and hope. We know loved ones and friends who are doing battle with disease. O Christ of the cross, let that bad news flower into the good news of health and mending. We know friends who are suffering from the emotional trauma of fractured relationships. For their sakes, we pray for mending; but if that is not possible, allow them to experience the invigoration of new self-confidence; the excitement of new challenges; the hope and joy of new relationships. Let them experience the truth that bad news is not the last word; that in you, good is possible in the midst of trying times.

We take our place beneath your cross, O Christ. And in so doing we remember your love and care for us, and we remember that evil and injustice and violence do not have the last say. For your yes to fullness of life is stronger than the world's no. Thank you for allowing us to see the whole of life through your gracious perspective. AMEN.

11 SECOND PRAYER IN MARCH

O GREAT Mystery! How is it that you choose to be wounded that we may have life? How is it, that with all your power, you choose to make us choose you? How is it that your plan for our wholeness stays the same even though we rebel against it; often ignore it? What inspires your patience with us; your long-suffering in our behalf; your willingness to steadfastly wait for us? O Sacred Head still wounded; thank you for your loving kindness; for your willingness to receive our perpetual conversions; for your open arms which welcome us whenever we turn home. O great mystery; help us to understand more than we have yet comprehended.

O Great Mystery! How is it that our lives are so interdependent? How is it that while we struggle so for independence, we must live in meaningful relationship or life is marked by emptiness and malaise? Why is it that we struggle so to find meaning in things when that which is really important is as near as a smile, a friendly arm, a hug, an encouraging word, a touch of love. Teach us how to tend to the important; how to make the most of that which really means the most.

O Great Mystery! As a part of our prayer we desire to lend our spiritual energy to the well being of persons who need our support. We pray for those who are recovering from sickness. Encourage them with improving health. We pray for those caught in the throes of important decisions. Speak to them in clear ways that they may decide in wisdom and in peace. We pray for those whose life seems full of the wrong things. Help them to empty out some of the frenzy, and give them the ability to take deep breaths in the freedom of new options. We pray for those in pain. Release them. We pray for those who feel threatened by age and the loss of energy; who wish to be as strong and vigorous as they used to be. Help them to use the gifts they have with purpose and joy.

O Great Mystery! A cardinal sings; a crocus peeps through the thawing crust; the sun grows stronger; and you are about to create all things new again. We rejoice in it. Through Christ we pray, AMEN.

THERE are some things we can do for ourselves, O God, but we are not good housekeepers of our hearts. We need your help. Create in us a clean heart, O God. Wash it free of the rust and tarnish of self interest, that we may be sensitive to those around us. Purge it of deceit and pretense, that all of our dealing may be marked by dependability and honesty. "Ret it up," that it may be free of old sin and a fitting place for good thoughts and ideas to be born and to live. Decorate it with laughter and love, that genuine joy might be daily fare for us.

Renew a right spirit within us, O God. We get so twisted out of shape by options and choices. We are haunted by our wants, unwilling to admit that, more often than not, when we have what we want we do not have what we need. We have trouble rejoicing in our blessings because we see others who are more blessed, and any setback to us is seen as betrayal on your part. Renew a right spirit within us, O God, that peevishness and anger and bitterness may no longer hold prime seats in our lives.

Cast us not away from your presence, O God. We need you when life tumbles in; when health is something we used to have; when pain becomes more than something someone else endures. We need you when fear of tomorrow is more than something we read in the newspaper. We need you when life gets mixed up and we can't make clean clear decisions about what to do.

Restore to us the joy of your salvation, O God.
Make us whole persons. Where there is illness give hope
in signs of improvement. Where there is loneliness send
the fullness of someone who cares. Where there is pain,
send release. Where there is depression, send a new sense
of self worth and optimism. Where there is boredom,
make us an offer to which we can't say no.

Uphold us with your free spirit, that we may have
strength to endure and liberty to rejoice and enjoy.
Through Christ we pray, AMEN.

13 FOURTH PRAYER IN MARCH
(Palm Sunday)

O LORD Jesus, as long ago you made your way to Jerusalem, so make your way this day into our hearts and lives.

Ride on, O Lord. Ride right into the fear and uncertainty we know in these days. The world crisis affirms with great intensity our need to be saved. When leaders of nations are reduced to name calling; charge and counter charge; threat and counter threat; we need some new model; some new king and kingdom for our allegiance. The kingdoms of our world seem unable to dwell in peace and mutual support. We confess, O Lord, to confusion and anger at human promises and human limitations and human decisions which create inhuman conditions. Ride into our lives with your love and concern for people, that our priorities may find again their pattern in your kind of good news.

Ride on, O Lord. Ride into the everyday routine of our lives. Bid us rejoice and celebrate all that enriches and renews and restores us. Help us to turn away from all that diminishes and limits and weakens us.

Ride on, O Lord. Ride into the needs of our lives. Ride into the emptiness, the perplexities, the unsureness. We do not ask that there be no pain or suffering, for if we could feel no pain, no sorrow, no shame, no loss; we would also feel no joy, no happiness, no fullness. But for all who suffer, we pray for release; for all who are in pain, we pray for relief; for all who are lonely we pray for relationship; for all who are trapped by circumstance, held prisoner by accident or disability, we pray for some experience of freedom. Weep for us in our humanness, O Lord, but stretch forth your healing hand and make us whole. Ride into our lives in such a way that the cup of life indeed overflows with power and hope.

Ride on, O Lord. Ride into our comfortableness and ease. Call us to bear your concern for the world; whether that be in bold decisions to conserve or share the resources of the earth; whether that be in commitment to your ministry to the hungry, the captive, the broken; whether it be in the difficult arena of labors for peace in the midst of international suspicion and violence; whether it be in the simple but demanding relationships of family and friends. If we must be armed in your name, let it be with a basin and a towel.

Ride on, O Lord. Ride again! We shall welcome you. Though at times your coming pains us; shames us; challenges us; we know you come in the interest of our healing and wholeness. Hosanna! AMEN.

14   FIFTH PRAYER IN MARCH
(Maundy Thursday Communion)

O GOD, you are the prime baker; the one who creates and supplies the staff of life; the great provider of bread; all kinds of bread for the world. Break to us the bread we need.

Break to us the bread of a grateful heart. How dry and scratchy the crumbs of peevishness are. How stale and hard the loaf of life becomes when we focus mostly on the disappointments; on the problems. How brittle and dry our portion when we have eyes which only see our neighbor's good fortune as one more blessing which passed us by. Break us the fresh bread of a thankful heart that recognizes joy and names it in grateful praise.

Break to us the bread of aliveness. We are alive, but the crust of hard routine stifles new growth. Our new ideas are more than a day old. Some of us can hardly remember a new commitment; a new beginning; a new offering of our lives and resources. Spring is coming, Lord. The call of the geese is an immediate prophesy. A brave pussy willow sticks its furry nose out of its winter sheath and tells us the earth is about to renew itself. Renew us, O Lord. Call us out of hibernation. By your grace, set aside the stale bread of what we have drifted into, and offer us the fresh bread of new beginnings.

Break to us the bread of peace. Not the moldy old bread of an eye for an eye; a tooth for a tooth. Offer us the sweet-smelling, warm, fresh-baked and buttered bread

of love that refuses to have enemies. Give us the peace
that comes with that kind of bread.

And finally, Lord, break to us the bread of healing.
Every broken heart needs mending; every grieving soul
needs the nourishment of healing; every pain-racked body
needs reprieve. By the power of your broken body, heal
all our unhealth. AMEN.

15 FIRST PRAYER IN APRIL
(Easter Sunrise)

THIS is a day you have made, O Lord. We will rejoice and be glad in it.

In some ways, it is a day like any other day; the sun comes up; light chases away darkness; the earth nourishes and things grow as the land keeps its own Easter; we wake to the same things yet we also wake to the possibility of new things. We give thanks for being a part of the routine of creation; for the chance to live in your creative cycle.

In some ways, it is a day like any other Sunday; true, some of us are up earlier, but then for some of us any getting up time is too early. Some of us will have a day of rest; some of us will have a day of catch up; for some of us it is a new day to face old problems—old pains, old hurts; for some of us it is a new day full of warm expectation with visiting family and loved ones.

We give thanks for this day and all it is; usual or unusual.

In some ways, it is a day unlike other days; for we give specialness to it as we remember with joy the gifts Christ made to us in the resurrection. All our days are different because of him. Faith and hope and love are the order of each day because of him. O God, bring to each of us the specialness of this day—a remembering which will inspire and renew us. Parade before our minds the strength and hope and joy of our faith. This is a day which you have made, O God. We will rejoice in it. Let the good news truly dawn upon us, that with gladness, we may join those around the world who joyfully shout, "He is risen indeed." AMEN.

16 SECOND PRAYER IN APRIL
(Easter)

O GOD, on this day; watchers, holy ones, bright seraphs, cherubim and throngs raise a glad strain of Alleluias. We want to join them. Even though the world is much the same as it was yesterday; even though there are still people suffering; even though millions are hungry; even though too many are trying to make war to create peace; even though there is much to worry us and dampen joy, despite all of that, this day we want to focus on good news. We want to sing with the gladness of those who celebrate the life you give in Jesus Christ. Give us the freedom this day to be rejoicing people.

O God, on this day there are among us many who do not feel glad. For them, life still has too much pain. Disease will not let them own too much hope. Some shrivel under the secret hurt of pieces of a broken heart. Some are angry in their loneliness. Some are worried about family. We pray for all such persons. We want better things for them. We ask you to touch them in their need. But on this day, we also want to be free to be glad; to rejoice in the promise of newness of life; to let our hope out of its prison; we want to be free to shout and make joyful Alleluias. For in the resurrection of Jesus, you have done great things for us. And we need to celebrate it.

O God, you know that we do not understand all there is to know about the resurrection. You know that we have questions; we have doubts; we want to believe; we do believe; we wonder about our own belief. But for this day, help us to understand just enough about what faith means, that we are willing to let faith be what it should be; deep conviction without proof, trust without protested guarantees; joy in a promise which does not have to be fulfilled before it can be enjoyed. This day we want to rejoice, to sing glad alleluias. Grant us the freedom to do so. AMEN.

17 THIRD PRAYER IN APRIL

O LORD, let not the joy of Easter fade so soon. Such Good News deserves to stay strong in our hearts; the dominant chord for all faith melodies; the standard to which all temporary suspensions must return. Bid us each bear our part in the songs of our salvation.

We are not huddled here in this room, with doors closed in worry that we will be held accountable for our gathering in your name. We have been blessed with the freedom to worship as we choose. Therefore we may worship, and we may do so without fear. But shall we sing, O Lord, before our faith is free of doubt? Or shall we wait until all questions are answered and our reason clearly sees the solution to every contradiction? Must our songs of praise wait until our logic is fully satisfied? No. Were we to do that, O God, our voices would forever be stilled. So free us to sing the goodness of Easter with faith unfinished. If we must start with simple tunes, abide with us until we can, in full harmony, bear our part in the sweet songs of salvation.

There are other things we must do besides enjoy our faith. We must seek your support for, and lend our spiritual energies to others. We think of those who find pain an everyday visitor; those who can hardly remember what it is to experience a hearty laugh; those who know the dread of malignancy, active or in remission; those who feel the hurt of shattered relationships. For all such poor in spirit, O God, save some special times of release; some moments of joy to let them know that life is still real; still a treasure.

Your creation is getting ready to explode with new life. There are brave beginnings everywhere, and they give us hope; and provide our doubting wintered souls with springtime beauty. Thank you for the offer of new life. Give us courage to see it; to reach for it; to accept it; to cherish it; and to enjoy it. Through Christ we pray. AMEN.

18 FOURTH PRAYER IN APRIL

CREATOR of the universe, and father and mother of each one of us; we have all prayed the same words, but as we prayed, we made our own applications and added our own particulars. No picture of you is more special, O God, than your open arms waiting to receive us after we have come to our senses. For equal treatment, for individual attention, for receiving us, accepting us, and sending us on our way refreshed, we give you thanks.

In our prayers, there comes to mind all who are held political or spiritual prisoners. Strengthen and protect and spare them. We remember those who feel violence is the only way a just cause will be recognized. Temper, mellow, or moderate them; that they may find a way to save face and still feel they have been heard. We remember current long-term conflicts, and pray for those who have lived for years with little more than hostility to mark their days. Sprinkle peace in little doses, Lord, for we are not used to too much at one time. But maybe we could learn.

For all who must endure pain, and feel the frustration and anger of that experience, open your arms of comfort to them. For all who feel the embarrassment and disappointment of broken relationships, open your arms of love and support. For all who feel wronged by another, and cannot forgive, and will not accept; open your arms, and in that pattern show them the way to wholeness. For all who wonder how to parent, how to be supportive of smart gifted youth who seem to want to be free without assuming responsibility, open your arms to demonstrate patience and listening, that in that pattern they may find strength. For all of us who forget how special a bright brisk day with spring waiting to spring is; how special clean air and daffodils and periwinkle and tulips are; and what a wonder it is to open our eyes to life and family and community, open your arms that with your blessing we may celebrate life and joy. Through Christ. AMEN.

19 FIFTH PRAYER IN APRIL

HOW SHALL our tongues adore thee, O Lord? You have created us special. As far as we know we alone, among your creatures, have been given the gift of joy and laughter. When we see the beautiful, we shall rejoice in it. When we hear marvelous musical sounds, we shall say so. When life is full to running over, blessed with fun and humor, we shall celebrate it; in little giggles; in chuckles; in snickers, in smiles of pleasure; in hearty laughter. We cannot adore thee laughing at others, but we can, laughing with them. We cannot adore thee if we are never serious, but we can praise you by refusing to take ourselves too seriously. Teach us how to purge ourselves of smallness; of withered and dried out vitality through the gift of laughter. Teach us how to adore you with the blessing of humor and smiles.

How shall our tongues adore thee, O Lord? We know they cannot praise while given to malicious speculation and idle tale bearing. We know they cannot praise when dedicated to the injury of another person. We know they cannot praise when committed to profanity or evil mischief. We know our tongues cannot praise you when they hedge or hide or bend from the truth. Teach us the gift of simple honest communication that we may praise you in our speech.

How shall our tongues adore thee, O Lord? They cannot praise you when narrowed down only toward our own interests. When we give them in concern for others, we have learned something about how to adore you. So we pray in these moments for others. You know who each of us has in mind, O Lord. Our prayer is for anyone who is lonely; for anyone who feels caught in circumstances which they do not know how to resolve; for anyone who wishes life could be more meaningful and exciting; for anyone who is faced with disease or disability or pain; for anyone impatient by slowness of recovery; for anyone broken in spirit. Grant that our tongues praise you in our intercessory prayer for those who have such special needs. Your presence working within them and in their behalf can make a difference. We ask it for their sake and in Jesus name. AMEN.

20   FIRST PRAYER IN MAY

O LORD GOD, standing as we are surrounded by all kinds of invitations and enticements; in the midst of a myriad of signposts and directions which bid us go here for joy and happiness and there for fun and pleasure; we confess our confusion and our need for some shepherding.

There is comfort in your promise to shepherd, O God. While we know by experience that you lead us in pleasant places; that you run our cup over with blessing; we also know by experience that we do not always go where we are led. Plagued with myopia and astigmatism, we see only what we want; and we convince ourselves that what we want is best for us. In the days which are ahead, make us less prone to argue against your way; less determined to insist on our own. Clear our vision, for what good is shepherding if those who need to be led refuse the shepherding.

There is also safety in your shepherding. Valleys and shadows come in many different forms and shapes. A mounting international crisis tempts us to flirt with war. As we flex our military muscles and rattle our swords, the shadows lengthen. Sometimes the shadowed valleys are closer home than foreign policy. A routine test shows a physical condition which threatens and requires extraordinary measures, and we are suddenly in the valley. Physical pain may weaken us; or emotional hurt may drain us; or anger at others or ourselves may consume our energy, and the shadows seem to envelope us. Brokenness at home, hurting or being hurt by those we love, or fear that those we love are wrecking their lives can put us in darkest valley. But there is safety and comfort in your leading. O Lord, if we can but remember to do all the best that we can and then in trust put the rest in your shepherd hands.

There are reminders of your love in those around us who love us and care for us. If we, as confused and uncertain as we are, know how to love and care for others, how much more there is for us from your shepherding. O good Shepherd, be present and welcome in our lives, for we desire that your goodness and mercy be the hallmark of our days. Through Christ we pray. AMEN.

21　SECOND PRAYER IN MAY

THE STRAINS of beautiful music soften the edges of our consciousness, rest our normal flutter over things undone, and give us welcome pause to think, to meditate, and be refreshed. We call to mind in these moments of meditation things related to family.

Lord God, mother and father of creation, we know that as a mother protectively gathers her young and as a father pities his children, so in love you fashioned the world and all that is in it; and in great love you gave your son that the world might have a true measure of lofty values and high morality, and a blessed means to salvation. We thank you for your parental love.

We thank you for mothers, who gave us our life through sharing their own when, before birth, we could not have lived without them. We thank you for the care we received when we could not care for ourselves, and for the preparation and training which enabled us to begin to assume responsibility for ourselves. We thank you for all the fond memories, the beautiful emotion, the deep feelings which are a part of remembering and experiencing mothers. And we pray for all women who feel inadequate, who feel oppressed, who feel harassed by the obligations of motherhood. Support them in their role and strengthen them for their charge.

We thank you for families where we learn accountability; honesty; trust; dependability; and love. They are our first friends. We thank you for all early training which fashioned the values which sustains community, within the family and within the world. We confess fears which make us wonder if the next generations will have the quality of human support which most of us knew. Give us wisdom to do all we can to encourage it.

Among us are some who find it hard to remember without experiencing pain. Comfort them. Among us are some who pray regularly to you that their family experience may be stronger, more secure, less threatening, bless them. Among us are some who, because of physical condition or forced change, find it hard to think of much else. Heal them and turn them loose for more creative things. AMEN.

O GOD, what a splendid place your spring world is. The red bud decorates the hills; the dogwood opens its pink and white pedals; the azaleas spread their passionate colors all over big and little bushes; and small things like violets and radishes begin to peep out of the ground. All around us is evidence of the beauty, the specialness, the importance of the right connections between vine and branch. We rejoice in the marvels of your world and the way creation graces our lives with beauty and practicality.

Why are we so quick, O God, to see the sensible in such connections, yet ignore those which mean so much to our own lives. We cut ourselves off from you, and lose a sense of wonder and mystery. We cut ourselves off from loved ones and family time, and can't figure out why we seem to be disoriented and dissatisfied. We cut ourselves off from times of unhurried contemplation and can't figure out why we don't get as many good ideas as we used to. We cut ourselves off from fellowship, and can't figure out why we don't seem as vital as we once were. We cut ourselves off from doing things for others, and can't figure out why we don't feel as good about who we are as we used to. Forgive us for our neglect and encourage us to choose more carefully the connections for our lives.

How good it is to celebrate our connections between one another. How good it is to renew old connections and make new ones. For all who travel safely and share the joys of hugging old friends and remembering good times, we thank you. For all who find new friends in unexpected places, we thank you.

There are among us those who carry unspoken burdens; those who face uncertain futures; those who shake hands everyday with pain; those who got up this morning hoping against hope that things would somehow miraculously change. Be their vine of strength and support, O God. There are among us those who bear the scars of broken relationships; those who wonder if they will ever trust love again. Be the vine of love which renews their trust, O God. There are those who would like the freedom to be in meaningful relationships, be the vine of new opportunity. Through the one true vine we pray, AMEN.

23 FOURTH PRAYER IN MAY

S PIRIT of God, descend upon our hearts. Wean them from earth; from all that enslaves or makes us prisoner; from all that keeps us from loving you with whole heart; from all that turns us away from service to selfishness. Stoop to our weakness, and in your might give us strength to endure pain, and reverses and adversity. Give us hope to replace uncertainty; faith to replace despair; confidence to replace doubt.

We ask no dream, no prophet ecstasy; no easy answer; no miracle that convinces against all questions; no angel visitant, no opening sky; no burning bush; no walk on the water; but take the dimness of our soul away that we may see you at work in the joy of human relationship; in human love which seeks not its own, which rejoices in the right, which is not peevish, which endures and never fails. Take the dimness of our soul away that we may see you at work in the simple kindness of one person to another, the grace of unearned service, the gift of caring one for another. Take the dimness of our soul away that we may rejoice in the coolness of a perfect summer day. Take the dimness of our soul away that we may, from the deep recesses of our heart, allow the pure pleasure of praise to pour forth.

We pray this day for our nation. We have so much to offer and are so short sighted in how to use it. We pray for the leaders of our nation. Give them wisdom beyond the normal answers. We pray for this congregation. Allow us, O God, to be a true community of faith where fellowship is more important than status; where caring is more important than comparison; where sharing is more important the receiving. We pray for those of our church family who are sick in body and soul; for those who suffer pain and disappointment; for those whose tears of frustration have dried up in hopelessness. We join now all those who pray for recovery. For those whose progress is slow or who pray not so much for recovery as for a plateau of stalled progression or remission, we add our prayerful support. Teach us to feel that you are always near.

Now get us ready for this day and for this new week. We wish to live it with the holy passion of your strength and love filling all our frame. Spirit of God, descend upon our hearts. AMEN.

O GOD, what shall we say to you on such a day. We can scarce protest the weather, for we have been blessed with cool nights to sleep; bright warm days in which to work or rest or revel in holiday events; and moisture enough for growing things to green the hills and fields. We shall simply rejoice in the joy and pleasure of such days and give you our thanks.

This holiday weekend not only whets our appetite for summer, for many it is a time of remembering. We remember persons who have moments of sadness and grief for those they have lost. We pray for them. Stir us all to new efforts at peace, that we never again easily succumb to the methodology of killing and being killed in order to preserve our liberty.

Because most of us enjoy the blessings of family or special friends at holiday celebrations, we remember those who are lonely and wonder if anyone cares. We remember those who feel broken from persons who mean the most to them. We remember those who are worried because loved ones seem to waste their precious ability and resources on life styles that can only end in disaster. Grant us, O Lord, the freedom to revel in the relation

ships which mean so much to us. Grant us to pray and
work wisely for loved ones who are lost and floundering.
And grant us sensitive hearts which reach out in care and
compassion for those who are poor in friends and loved
ones.

O God, there are some sick enough to feel their
whole life is preoccupied with health; there are some who
find love threatened by brokenness; there are some who
experience holiday as more hassle than relaxation; there
are some whose face would hurt if they could smile;
there are some who have little to which they can look
forward. To all such, O God, grant your special favor.
Let newness grace their lives.

You carry in your heart, O God, a concern for the
peace and well being of your creation and all your creatures. Immerse in your blessing all efforts at establishing
new foundations for peace in our world. Whether they
know it or not, infuse some of your peace into all men
and women who are world leaders. Through Christ we
pray, AMEN.

25   FIRST PRAYER IN JUNE

O LORD GOD, creator of blue skies, green trees, and bright flowers; creator of grey skies, gypsy moths, crab grass, and incurable disease; O Lord God, creator of great women and men; creator of violent men and women; we stand with grateful hearts in the presence of beautiful benevolent creation—we stand with perplexed hearts in the face of destructive creation. Yet through what seems like inconsistency, we catch the thread of loving purpose; unanswered questions do not discourage us; suffering will not tempt us to unfaithfulness; we know we have our place in your grand design. Let us abide there in joy and peace.

Sometimes, O God, we long for wings to fly to the wilderness of uninvolvement—to the desert of freedom from our neighbors need. Give us no wings for such a journey for without our neighbor we are deprived of a part of you.

Sometimes we long to fly where there are no giants to test our courage. Give us no wings for such a journey for we grow and toughen with challenges.

Sometimes, O God, we long for wings to fly from

family and friends to new surroundings where old scars
and old memories do not unfairly mark us. Give us no
wings for such a journey, for who we are goes with us;
and surgical escape is seldom as strong as mending relationships.

If we pray for wings, O God, grant us wings to soar
gently, strongly, playfully, purposefully. Grant us wings
to fly in the face of challenge, to glide comfortably on
the updraft of mystery, to dart and dive and flit away
from danger. Grant us wings to travel when we should,
and wings to fold when it is time to rest.

O Lord, we are special only because you make us
special in your love. Hear the prayer of your people
gathered in this place today. Some come weary with the
same prayer—some come timid with a new prayer.
Some come in pain—some in joy. Some come in fear-
—some in anticipation. Some come in faith—some in
doubt. However we come, hear us—respond to us in
Jesus name.

We pray together now as you taught us to pray . . .

26 SECOND PRAYER IN JUNE

O LORD, our days seem like some tossed salad with mixed ingredients of joy and pain. We pause to let the joy of a multi-colored green tree refresh our soul and the squeeze of next month's bills flits through our mind. We sit down to a sumptuous meal, and as we relish the good smell and taste, images of starving persons flash through our minds. We gather in beautiful summer days with loved ones and friends, and in the midst of that joy we remember the lonely and the hostage. Your word tells us that we cannot go where you are not, O Lord. Help us to know your presence in the mixed ingredients of life.

Let no giants terrify us, O God. Receive us, hear us, minister to us, that we may not hide or run from the rigors of life. And bless us, that there may be times of pure joy and goodness and laughter.

God, our lives are also filled with commitments and mistakes; with service to others and selfishness; with good intentions and bad ideas. Leave us not to ourselves; do not allow us to go where we think you will not be. For if your presence makes us uncomfortable, Lord, it is of our own doing. So teach us how to receive the discomfort as reminders and warning, and if that presence is a blessing, teach us how to trust it and rejoice in it.

Now, Lord, hear those who are praying their own concerns. Hear those who are troubled; those who wonder if anything will ever be different; those who can't find the right direction for life; those who wonder if there are yet things of importance for them to do. Hear those who are in pain; those who are happy and do not know where to direct their thanks. Hear those who come to you as old friends, and those who are afraid to come because they do not know what to say or do. O Lord, leave us not to ourselves, for we cannot in our own strength make this life what you created it to be. AMEN.

27 THIRD PRAYER IN JUNE

S OME days, O God, we feel like singing a marvelous
song of praise. Some days we notice the blue sky; the
flit of the debonair blue jay; the nervous hustle of the
squirrel; and music of joy wells up in us. Some days we
hum a little tune of contentment before we ever think
about it. Some days there is a flash of peace, a sense of
fulfillment in a completed task. Some days, joy in the
love and fellowship which is a part of our lives just
washes us clean of all other grubbiness, and the beginnings of a bright song of praise bubbles up within us. For
all days when we can smile and sing in joy and peace we
give you thanks.

But days when we rend our garments come to us.
Days when our ledger of goodness seems to be bankrupt;
days when a song of joy would seem a mockery; days
when words of praise and thanksgiving almost turn sour
in our mouths. O God, when we are disappointed, worn
down, angry, tired; when there isn't a single note in our
heart which smacks of belonging to some marvelous
song; O God, on those days, accept us, love us, give us
strength, abide with us, until there is a release and we can
see life again in a more balanced perspective.

We meet together, O God, and there is strength and comfortableness and goodness in that togetherness. Teach us how to cultivate togetherness by being sensitive and encouraging to one another. Save us from injuring another with our tongue. Slow our speech that we have time to think so that our words do not abuse. Encourage our abilities toward kindness. And when we ourselves are injured by a brother or sister, give us grace to share the hurt that by common effort we may mend the brokenness.

Teach us, O God, how to celebrate our togetherness by being open to the needs and concerns of those around us; by being willing to listen to one another; by being willing to accept one another as we receive acceptance from you. So shall our lives know strength and peace. And the way we live together may be a song of joy. AMEN.

28   FOURTH PRAYER IN JUNE

O GOD of the day and the night; of cloudy days and sunlit skies; God of the cold north wind and the soft tropical breeze; you are above all and in all. And yet you invite us, everyone, into deep relationship with you.

When we come to you in prayer we come shyly. We don't know how to say the right things. We can't seem to find words that sound right or that will make proper prayers. We are afraid we can't pray like others who do it so well. Yet you welcome us; timid, faltering, inarticulate; you encourage our stuttering; you hear our deepest feelings and understand our hearts. We give you thanks.

When we come to you in prayer, we come uncertainly. Piled up in our memory are the good intentions never completed; the resolutions broken; the petty irritations nurtured; the anger enjoyed; the willful mistakes; the stupid jealousies and our list of unkindnesses to pay back. O God, we have them all, yet you welcome us, bid us be repentant and receive forgiveness and life and health and wholeness. We thank you that forgiveness is not a mystery we have never known.

When we come to you in prayer, we come overwhelmed. There is such suffering and anxiety, by many

who have no work. There is so much sickness, despair of
spirit and disease of body. There is so much fear of the
power of others; so much commitment to violence as the
way to protect ourselves. There is so much loneliness, so
much brokenness, so much lostness. How can we be at
peace when we are surrounded by so much which is
unpeaceful. Yet you bid us welcome to a strength and
wholeness which the world cannot give nor take away.
We thank you. And with whatever strength we have, we
give our spiritual energies in support of persons who have
special needs whom we name to you in these moments of
quiet.

This time each week with you is precious, for somehow it puts in perspective our shyness, our weakness, our
fear, our pain and suffering, our frustration, and our
thanksgiving. Grant that your promises of regeneration
and newness and wholeness may be more than a hope,
more than a wish. Make us open and receptive that it
may be unto us as you have promised. In Jesus name we
have prayed.

29   FIRST PRAYER IN JULY

HOW can we rest in you, O Lord, when there is so much that needs to be done? You would not want us to be lazy, would you Lord? There are the hungry of the world; the oppressed; the poor. How can we rest when there is so much injustice, so much need, so much violence? Teach us that in rest there is renewed strength for what needs to be done, and when we learn that lesson, grant us rest.

How can we rest in you, O Lord, when even our rest is restless? Full calendars are a life style with us. Oft times we choose busyness so that we don't have to deal with unpleasantness or persons we'd rather not face. How can we rest when it gives us time to think and understand what we're doing? Being forced by busyness is easier than thoughtful choice. Teach us that in rest there is new perspective and courage for what should to be done, and when we learn that lesson, grant us rest.

How can we rest, O Lord? The news is seldom good. Nations bristle; races clash; natural disaster strikes; people in public office laugh at morality; a loved one is making a mistake; a lab test threatens us with dreaded news. How can we rest when there is so much that caus es us fear. Teach us, O God, that resting in you is more than idling our gears; it is more than "forgetting it all." It is an exercise of trust and patient choice. When we have learned that lesson, grant us rest.

How can we rest, O Lord? Your beautiful earth is cracked and dry and calls out for the blessing of rain. Green things are brown, growing things are withering, developing things are stunted. We have waited patiently, then impatiently. There are many whose livelihood rests in falling rain. Take pity, O Lord, and bless your parched earth with the gift of moisture.

How can we rest in you, O Lord, when it seems a waste of time to rest. Teach us that rest is more than doing nothing. Show us that rest is creative time; energizing time; recovery time; renewal time; thanksgiving time. And when we have learned our lesson, grant us rest. Through Christ we pray, AMEN.

30 SECOND PRAYER IN JULY

O GOD, sometimes we do not want you by our side. Sometimes we say we want to be left alone. We want to be free to be what we want to be; to do what we want to do. Sometimes having you by our side feels oppressive; like a policeman or an untrusting parent. At such times, O God, do not depart from us, for the problem is a problem we have with ourselves, not with you. We know, in our better moments, that you want only our good. Do not take a vacation from us, Lord. Do not leave us alone. In the eternal battle between good and evil; between right and wrong, we want you on our side.

Give us friends and loved ones to be by our side, O God. Life is also relationship, and in loving and being loved there is a wholeness with which aloneness can never compete. Though privacy is at times a grace, we are people who need people to make life whole. Grant us sustaining and supportive relationships. And make us persons who know whom to give friendship and love.

There are among us persons who specially need to feel you care. Wherever someone feels by themselves, make your presence known. Wherever someone faces a tough decision which can only be made in the intimacy of their own heart, be by their side. Wherever someone must live with pain, be by their side to comfort and give release. Wherever someone must have time for anger to subside, be by their side. Wherever someone wants to reach out in an effort to heal a brokenness or a hurt, be by their side. Wherever someone wants to sing a glad song of praise or thanksgiving; wherever someone wants to acknowledge that life's cup runs over with a thousand blessings, give them a merry tune and sing it side by side with them.

There is much suffering in our world, Lord. We dare not cry out, "Why don't you do something about the hungry starving people in the world," because you might ask us a question like, "Why don't you?" There are some needs over which we have no control. Help us when you can, O Lord, but do not help us at the expense of our neighbors. In Jesus' name we have prayed. AMEN.

31 THIRD PRAYER IN JULY

BREAK thou true bread for us, O Lord. Not some tasty morsel which teases the tongue but leaves us hungry. Not something pleasurable to the palate but sterile of substance and nurture. We need real bread that will energize and sustain life. We pray to have it broken to us.

We are not good at choosing for ourselves, O Lord. Your table is bountifully filled with things of peace. Still we pass along life's smorgasbord and find weapons, and war; confrontation and threat. And it seems good. Break to us the true bread of peace.

We are not good at choosing for ourselves, O Lord. Your table is filled with true community. Still we pass along and find at other tables enticing things which separate and divide; we suspect the worst about our neighbors and pass along our concern only to have it become fact in someone else's mind. And a friend suffers from our assumptions, and our loose tongue. Someone we know hurts and we are afraid to get involved; we don't have the time. And community is fractured because we chose the bread of uninvolvement. Someone raises the same old concern we've heard a hundred times, and we turn away, wearied of the repetition. And community is broken because we refuse to really listen. We choose brokenness and long for real relationship. Break to us the true bread of community, O Lord.

We are not good at choosing for ourselves, O Lord. Your table is filled with compassion and care and strength. But we choose to fill our plates with discouragement and depression and disillusionment. We think what we want would be satisfying. If all could be as we say it should be, we would be happy. But it is not so. Give us a portion of true bread which lets us lean on your will and your blessing and your plan with confidence and trust.

Among us are those whose bodies place real burdens on their spirit. Break to them the bread of courage and hope. Turn around all that can be turned around, and give strength and comfort where disease and hurt still abide.

Among us are those who have lost loved ones. Break to them the bread of compassion and love to combat loneliness and loss.

Among us are those who feel the pressure of too much to do; give to them the bread which provides a restful break. We all hunger and thirst for righteousness; but we are poor choosers. Break to us what we truly need. Amen.

S WEET hour of prayer, that calls us from a world of care. We are a busy people, O God, who seldom take time to count our blessings as real treasures and rarely wait and listen in your presence. It is good to do so. Still, O God, we do not desire that our prayer ignore the world or its care. Our times are beset with racial strife, big stick diplomacy, and precarious play on the edge of nuclear annihilation. Can it please you if we only wring our hands and say, "What can we do?" Can it please you if we shrug our shoulders and say, "It's the way the world is?" Can it please you that a large portion of the world's people would choose to die because negotiating seems weaker than fighting. If we are not uneasy, not frightened by all of this, do not allow our hour of prayer to be sweet. Stir up in us some portion of holy outrage; some last straw that bids us take action and stance which begins to contribute to peace.

Sweet hour of prayer. In season of distress and grief, our souls have often found release. Among us are those who carry the scars of shattered relationships; among us are those whose loved ones live on borrowed time; among us are those who rejoice when there is five minutes without pain; among us are those who sense the growing shadow of their own mortality. O God, we pray for wholeness and health for those who don't have it. And, O God, we pray for godly strength and spiritual courage for those who can't have wholeness and health. And if it be our calling to serve and encourage or minister to someone in need, save us from turning away or being preoccupied.

Sweet hour of prayer, thy wings shall our petition bear. We pray for those we love who are dear to us; we pray for those we do not love; opponents, competitive colleagues; enemies; the unforgiving with long memories. We pray for ourselves, for we know how bitterness, revenge, and hostile getting even belittles us. Help us learn the lessons of genuine forgiveness that peace and joy may not only be a vision of that which is to be, but also something which is with us and in us. Through Christ we pray. Amen.

33 FIRST PRAYER IN AUGUST

LET THERE be praise and joy in our hearts, O God. We have so many suggestions about how things could be different and better. It could be cooler; there could be more rain; we could be less busy; we could have more vacation; we could have fewer bills to pay. The unfortunate we smart over, the good we take for granted. Forgive us when we fret so much about the way things aren't that we forget to be thankful for the remarkable blessings which are ours in the way things are.

In these moments we will remember enough to let there be praise and joy in our hearts. Call to our mind the joy of a good stretch when we've slept soundly; the exhilaration of a day when we don't have to follow a regular routine, the grace of a drink of cold water going down on a hot day. Review for us the pleasure in the song of the thrush; the sight of the hovering hummingbird's miraculous flight; the nervous chittering of the squirrels. Call to our mind the good feeling when we are comfortable with a loved one; the excitement when we look forward to being with friends or family; the wonder of mutual love creating a new baby; the richness of watching children grow and mature, the full heart experienced when a child says, "I love you grandpa." The list is longer than we can finish. We have enough and more for there to be joy and praise in our hearts. Let it be, dear Lord.

We do not desire to gloss over the pain and hurt which is a part of life. We know persons who are bowed down with heavy responsibilities; persons who are trying to gather the pieces of broken relationships; persons who wonder what it would be like to feel healthy again; persons who both accept and struggle against physical limitations. By your spirit, Lord, when any of us we are confused or in pain, we are able to live in strength and courage if, in faith, we remember and ask for help. Let it be so for all who need you. Let some sense of blessing touch each one who joins in this prayer. And in return, you shall hear in our hearts a song of praise and joy. Through Christ we pray, Amen.

34 SECOND PRAYER IN AUGUST

LORD GOD, when we stand on the edge of our own wilderness, deciding whether to go forward or fall back, who stands with us? Who protects us in our wanderings; who guides us when the way is uncertain; who sustains us when we are weary and discouraged; who cautions us when we are ready to betray ourselves and others; who strengthens our hand when we are weak? Surely, only you, O God, faithfully meet us at life's busiest and most crucial intersections. We confess how important you are in our lives.

Lord God, who makes our soul sing with little melodies of pleasure; who gives the joy of colorful sunsets and soft nights; who blesses our spirit with the wonder of musical sound; who touches us with the grace of human love in families or friends; who generates within us the goodness of a thankful heart; who inspires us to compassion and care of others; who helps us applaud those moments when we are our best selves? Surely, only you, O God, faithfully meet us at life's most happy and blessed experiences and regularly encourage us to celebrate the goodness of life.

Lord God, our prayer reaches out to those around the world who do not have their daily bread. We pray for all those who live each day in the middle of violence.

We pray for all those who are oppressed and betrayed by power and politics. We pray for all who are bowed down with pain and disease. We pray for all those worn out by the same problems they had to bare last week . . . last year. We pray for those who are unhappy with themselves and don't know how to fix their own lives. O God, stand all your frustrated and suffering servants on the edge of some promised land, and when it is our turn to stand there, let us not turn away in fear or anger. Let our footsteps neither falter nor stray. You are with us. Who can be against us? You guide our steps, who can mislead us? You point our way, who can lose us? Lord God, thank you for giving us the potential of new life in the disguise of risk; new opportunity in the offer to leave the old; and your presence to go with us. You renew our hope and our purpose. Thank you. Amen.

35 THIRD PRAYER IN AUGUST

GOD of the hot and the humid, the cool and the clear; God of the dry and parched, the wet and nourished; God of mowed-down, moist hay and standing ready grain; God of left-over strawberries and still- green raspberries; our days are in your hands. Teach us to be patient with the schedules and alterations of your creation. For if we wait in faithfulness, we will have our daily bread and to spare, and our cup will surely run over.

God of mirth and joy; of little smiles and hearty laughter; thank you for funny things; for lighthearted things; for things that make us snicker and things that make us grin. When you created us in your image, thank you for giving us a part of your sense of humor. Thank you for the wonderful release and well-being which comes from good laughter, and thank you for filling life with joy.

God of pain and suffering, God of disappointment and disillusionment, God of broken hearts and fractured relationships, God of medical tests that scare us with their reports and surgeries that don't do enough to give us a clean bill of health, and God of diseases which hang on with dreadful monotony; be with us in our human frailty.

Show us the fine line between trustful dependency on your grace, and the willingness to do battle against that which would seem to threaten to undo us, that we may live in faith and at the same time do all we can to help ourselves.

God of the church; of small and large groups; God of two or three gathered together in your name and God of hundreds waiting before you in prayer; God of those who hunger and thirst for righteousness and of those who have turned to more exciting but less fulfilling menus; put the hand of your blessing upon this church, that, anointed with your strength and power, she may be the means of young and old finding their lives under your kingship and rule. Through Christ we pray, AMEN.

36 FOURTH PRAYER IN AUGUST

O GOD, we are surrounded by a cacophony of sounds which bombard our senses. There are raucous sounds which bid us celebrate less than our best; enticing sounds which invite us to squander our resources for the temporary or cheap; there are soft sounds of deceit, boisterous sounds of privilege; rumbling sounds of national security and military might, and there is always the uneven beat of prejudice and injustice. But like the clean, clear, unwavering sound of the trumpet, your voice comes through if we listen and recognize. Play for us the songs of truth, and noble purpose; the melodies of human kindness.

O God, the sounds of joy seem so few to many of us. The ripple of giggles and chuckles, the explosion of hearty laughter, the relaxation of a broad smile; they all seem too much a stranger in our lives. We know the heavy sounds of pain; the fretful sounds of worry; the repetitious sounds of anxiety. We know the uncertain melody of disease, the familiar tune of troubled loved ones, and the monotonous notes of slow recovery. If we listen, your presence comes through like the soft penetrating sound of the trumpet. We pray that all those who need a touch of joy and confidence in their lives may hear the trumpet of your strength and comfort.

O God, the melodies of our life seem somehow sloppy and mushy; run together; fast paced but loose and imprecise. Like an expert triple tongue, bring melodious clarity to our lives.

O God, we start so many things we don't finish. We spread the notes of good intentions around, but can't seem to find time to fit them together and finish the song. Like an expert horn player, lead us from one good note to the next that starting and finishing may be a familiar theme.

O God, we are such slow learners. We know how to carry a big stick and make people afraid, but we have not learned how to blast out and hold the high notes of peace and good will which preserve meaningful relationships. In the orchestra of our lives we see enemies instead of friends, strangers instead of colleagues, competitors instead of loved ones. Like the clean clear voice of the trumpet, set us straight. Amen

37   FIRST PRAYER IN SEPTEMBER

LORD of all being, throned afar; your glory flames from sunset and twinkling star; from bird song and thunder roll; from delicate flower petal and rock- ribbed mountain ridge; from the boundary of this earth to the infinity of the universe. Center and soul of every sphere, yet to each loving heart how near. For your glory is surely in the infectious laughter of a happy child; in the supportive touch of a friend; in the look of a loved one; and in the gift of care shared between one person and another. Thank you, O God, for all the marvelous and beautiful things we see and feel which share the wonder of who you are.

We think our dark time is your smile withdrawn. But not every midnight is your frown of disapproval or judgment. Our bodies are weak; they grow older, and the frailness of our flesh becomes subject to disease, painful and restrictive. But the strength and comfort of your love is still with us. We choose the wrong; revel in the unimportant; neglect the significant; but even in the night of such resistance, the light of your love prevails, for no darkness we choose can overcome it. Forgive our waywardness and our indifference, and accept our joyful thanks for your rainbow arch which cheers the long watches of the night.

Lord of all being, far above yet very near, be close beside all those who grieve the loss of love, either because of death or because of broken relationships. Be with all who are afraid, because they do not trust the future or because they have sown seed which they do not want to harvest. Be with all who are lonely and yearn for the ears of someone who will listen and share the wonder of life and relationship. Be with all who wish for meaning and fulfillment in life and keep coming up short on supplies of joy and purpose.

Lord of all being, we assign certain persons with more responsibility than seems fair. Be beside the leaders of nations whom we charge with the survival of peace, the custody of our common good, and the protection of human rights. Through Jesus Christ we pray. Amen.

38 SECOND PRAYER IN SEPTEMBER

WELCOME to prayer, O God. But not without some problem. The indictment, "neither hot nor cold" rankles us a bit. Hasn't the world taught us not to be too involved? Can we afford to be hot or cold on issues like disarmament, or world hunger, or discrimination, or injustice? Have we not learned that some things are beyond our control—that there are some things we can't do anything about? Why should you feel upset, O God, when our being hot or cold seems to make so little difference?

Ah, but we speak in circles, O God. There are some things we get hot and cold about, whether they are practical or not; whether they work or not. See how hot we get over the snub of a friend; see how upset we get when someone says something we don't like; see how cold we get when we feel unappreciated; see how angry we get when some insensitive person takes advantage of us. O yes, O Lord, we are hot and cold people. We give our support to our children, whether they choose what we would choose or not. We are passionate about them whether they become who we wanted them to be or not. We love another whether the person is always their best or not. Hot and cold feelings are a part of every decision we make which requires any form of commitment.

O God, the indictment stands. But we do not want to be apathetic people. Grant us the passion of genuine commitment. Teach us the joy of energetic involvement. Bless us with caring spirits which reach out to others. Baptize us, three times over, with joy and happiness. Save us from being indifferent. Sensitize us. Revitalize us. We want to be people who feel, who get hot or cold, who know pain and pleasure.

And so in our prayer, we want to reach out to those who need special support. We pray for any who face the pain and uncertainty of illness; for any who are broken in spirit; for any who wish that tomorrow would be different from today. We pray for those who are unhappy and don't know how to get outside of themselves; and for those who are happy and can't celebrate. We pray for any who feel half whole and wish to be complete. And we pray it all in the name of Christ. Amen.

O GOD, though some of us are embarrassed by the sound of our own voices; though some of us confess we cannot carry a tune in a bucket; never the less, by the encouragement of your Word we are persuaded to sing a new song to the Lord. In the privacy of these moments, we will seek to come before you with a voice of singing.

We shall sing in awe at the potency of nature. How dwarfed are our efforts at power when we are in the path of a hurricane. How helpless we feel in the face of a hundred-thousand-acre forest fire. Be with those who have suffered from nature's terror, and bless those who have risked life and resources as they offered help and shelter.

We shall sing in amazement at the wonder and mystery of your creation. How do the trees know when to change their clothes? Why do they all do it together in season? How do the squirrels know they must stash away their winter's food when the days are still so beautiful? How do so many living things know they must rest before life begins again in newness and vigor? What keeps life within a seed until it germinates? How do forces within our own body know when to fight infection and disease? We think we know some answers, but the initiation and continuing design of it all is a marvel. With a voice of singing, we rejoice in the order and dependability of creation.

We shall sing in behalf of brothers and sisters who need our support. Some among us have lost loved ones. Some keep patient and helpless vigil with family members who may never be normal again. Some bear the scars of broken hearts, for which there seems no helpful cure. Some have lost their way and cannot, in their own strength, find themselves. Some need simple fortitude for the tasks of the day; whether that be in home, or work, or in school. With a voice of singing, we pray that your spirit may encourage and strengthen each one according to their need.

With a voice of singing, we declare this and desire it to be heard, O God: that our lives are fuller, richer, and securer because you are our God and we are your children. Complete our prayer as we pray together as our Lord taught us to pray . . .

B OW DOWN thine ear, O Lord, not because we speak from distance, but because we speak from difference; not as one completely other, but as one who, incarnate in Christ, stands with us, yet is also far above us. We ask you to bow down, not to keep us from shouting in anger, (though sometimes we do), but so we may speak softly, intimately; so we may be able, as your son Jesus bid us, to say "Abba Father," Daddy—Papa!

Bow down thine ear, O Lord, and hear our perplexity. Fear seems to be stronger than love. Power seems to work better than caring. Defense seems to be more trusted than diplomacy. War is studied more than peace. Individuality seems more workable than interdependence. Nations and churches and families have trouble living according to the way of your son. O Divine Papa, encourage us. Save us from fainting or growing weary in the way. Keep us from giving up on love and service.

Bow down thine ear, O Lord. You have told us that as "one whom a mother comforts, so you will comfort us." We want to whisper our care and concern. Some of us are battling uncertain illness. Some of us are fighting temptations to give in and give up. Some of us see tomorrow as uncertain, perhaps a day for a pink slip that hangs the big U of unemployment on our back. Some of us work with no joy. Some of us bear the pain of brokenness from family and friends. Some of us stand in a moment of decision and are not sure which way to go. O Divine Mama, put your arms around us, and hold us, and love us, and help us.

Bow down thine ear, O Lord, for we also want to whisper sweet somethings in your ear. Life is a treasure or we would not fret so. We thank you for it; and for all that life brings of love and joy and laughter and warmth and caring and sharing; for all it brings of beauty in sight and sound. O divine parent of the world, bow down and we shall put our arms around you in thanksgiving and joy, and we shall laugh a little, and cry a little, and ask forgiveness, and make promises, and go our way refreshed and strengthened.

Bow down, O Lord, and we shall finish our prayer as you taught us to pray, Our Father . . .

41   FIRST PRAYER IN OCTOBER

O GOD, you are the same yesterday and today and forever, yet you promote and encourage change. The sun shortens its stay each day, and already some of the more fashion conscious trees have begun to shed their old clothes and put on the bright colors of fall. The squirrels and birds are getting ready. Change will come. But in the change we see divine purpose and dependability; a hope for the new. O God of natural change, grant humankind the promise of change.

We love the secure, O God. We are more prone to leaving things the way they are than to changing. Still, we carry in our heart the hope that things may be different; that warfare might be more unusual and peacefulness more usual; that dishonesty might give way to integrity; that kindness might become more important than selfishness; that wisdom might be more sought than knowledge; that love might be a joy experienced by every human being. O God of change, make us open to change.

O God of change, we pray for all who secretly hope for change. For those who want sickness to be overcome by health; for those who want pain to cease and infection to disappear, grant change. For families who are at their wits end with one another; for persons who long to be in relationship but are lonely, grant change. For all who know what they should do and can't seem to do it; persons bound by consuming habits; students locked into study procrastination; any of us with good intentions which gather like old books lining the shelves of our days. O God, grant change.

O God, give us grace to change enough that we can also be thankful. There are daily joys we take for granted that should be noted. So we give you thanks for the blessing that comes from a good sneeze, from a hearty laugh, from tears of joy. We give you thanks for the promise of new life in little babies, and vigorous youth, and hope for new beginnings in those of well-worn days. O God of change, grant some to each of us, in the name of Jesus we pray. Amen.

L OVER of the children; make us childlike too.
    Make us childlike in our faith,
        in our trust,
            in our hope,
                in our optimism,
    Make us childlike in our enthusiasm,
        our joy,
            our curiosity,
                our desire to learn,
    Make us young again, that we may still have room
    to grow and mature and ripen.

Lover of the children, save us from being childish,
    in our relationships,
        in our disagreements
            in our anger,
                in our demands.

    Save us from being childish,
        in our insensitivity,
            in unwillingness to assume responsibility,
                in our jealousy and envy,
                    in our stubbornness,
                        in our vengeance.

Lover of the children, help us to be childlike without being childish.

O God, there is more that is childish than is child like in our international scene. Today people are dying because we've made schoolyard reasoning the basis for international relationships. When the best reason we can give for a war is "We didn't start it," then our government is operating with little more than juvenile sandbox diplomacy. O God, how childish it is when we make who started the fight more important than who will have the wisdom and maturity to prevent needless loss of lives. O God, let someone with childlike honesty call the war what it is; an obscene game that represents the worst in those old enough to be more than childish.

O God, we are all children in your eyes. Some of us hurt from loss of a loved one; some of us hurt because we are half of a broken relationship. Some of us hurt because we feel alienated and don't know how, or won't work at reconciliation. Some of us are in physical pain; some in mental anguish. Lover of the children, find some way to share your love with all your children who need support and strength. AMEN.

43 THIRD PRAYER IN OCTOBER

(The Congregation was invited to lay their hands in their laps, close their eyes, and clench both fists. Then slowly turn their hands up and open them.)

HERE are our open hands, Father. Take our hand and lead us. The maps we have been given by the world are not trustworthy. If we go the way we are instructed to go, we do not arrive at the place we've been promised. And the travel is full of danger and detours. Take our hand that we may go safely in green pastures.

Take our hand and lead us, Father. As a congregation, we need to be encouraged to do our going with faithfulness and energy. We want to both be in mission and be nurtured. We want to find a way to be a blessing to others and a way for life to have meaning and purpose. Take our hand that we may fully be able to do both.

Take our hand and lead us, Father. Life is a blessed gift, not a test. It is a treasure, not a punishment. We shall have pain and disappointment and heartbreak, but that is because we are mortal; we do wear out; we do make mistakes; we are vulnerable. But if you have us in your hand, we can endure without disillusionment; we can be safe even though we may be worried; we can be confident even though there is uncertainty, we can wait for an answer even though we don't see how anything can be done. Keep hold of us Lord.

Take our hand and lead us, Father. As we go with you, show us the bright colors and the soft autumn sun. Show us the flowers which have not yet succumbed to the frost. Show us the red berries which nurture the birds and the falling acorns which are support for the squirrels. Show us the dogwood buds wrapped in little green cases waiting for spring. Take our hand, Lord, and show us the care and companionship of those who love us. Show us the sympathy and compassion of neighbors. Show us the touch of support; the glisten of a tear; the squeeze of a hug which means we are not alone. Show us smiles of joy. For if you have our hand, O God, we see life in a different way, and we behold so much more than if we walk alone.

We know that life will catch up with us, and before we know it, our fists will be clenched again. But thanks for this time of opened handed conversation. We have prayed in Jesus name, Amen.

J ESUS, son of David, have mercy on us. We have eyes to see, but we are blind to too much. Around us are persons, sore in heart and soul, who could use support and comfort, and we are too busy to see them. Around us are neighbors who have brokenness in their homes and family relationships, and we turn our eyes the other way. Around us are persons who do not have the necessities for very simple living, and we choose to see more clearly the things we want that we do not yet have. Give us our sight, Lord, that we may be more aware of those around us who need our neighborliness.

Jesus, son of David, have mercy on us. We sometimes see more than we should see. Seven hours a day of TV with real and fictional violence; the color of someone's skin which allows us to label and stereotype; the length or style of someone's hair which tells us what kind of person they are; the way a person dresses which tells us whether they are our kind or not. Give us sight, O Lord, that we may see in every person your face; for whatever we do to or think about anyone—we do to you.

Jesus, son of David, have mercy on us. We walk in the splendor of fall and forget to celebrate it because of the trash someone has thrown on the street. We live in the love of those who care about us, and instead of rejoicing in it we worry about things we see, over which we have no control. Bless us with vision which allows us to see joy and rejoice in it.

Jesus, son of David, have mercy on all who need your special care; the sick, the injured, the alone, the frustrated, the hurt, the brokenhearted, the lost; have mercy on the insensitive, the calloused, the aloof; have mercy on the bored, the beaten, those who hunger and thirst for righteousness.

Jesus, son of David, giver of sight, give us clear vision; that tomorrow may learn from today without being controlled by it; give us clear vision that truth may always be visible beneath the glitter and gloss of popular wisdom; give us clear vision that peace may be a real way to live rather than a disappointing dream. In your name we pray. Amen.

O LORD of all things and giver of life, you are our sure foundation. Years ago, you told us if we do the things you say, our lives will be built on a rock; and if not, then we are on shaky ground. Knowing that, we manage to ignore it in many ways. Is it not strange, Lord, that we will spend hours studying a book on how to master some new technological marvel that saves us time, but we give very little time to having some new thought or idea to strengthen and renew our faith. Is it not strange Lord, that what we could be doing in spirit by slow but sure and steady growth we wait to do in the face of some crisis? Save us from such foolishness. Last night we changed our clocks, for it was the season to fall back in time. But it is never the season to fall back in the faith. Give us wisdom to accept and tend the sure foundation you have made for us.

We ask you to hear our prayers for those among us who need special care, for individuals who face serious surgery, for others who remain on our prayer list because their health makes them a prisoner to uncertainty and pain. And we pray for the quiet unknown suffering and brokenness and disenchantment which hides behind our everyday faces. Among us are relationships which need mending; things said which need forgiveness; choices which need direction; loved ones who need support. Bless each one who reaches out for strength and wisdom. Become a recovered foundation for them. And where we can be of help, grant us the ability to point to and represent some of your strength as we see and respond.

Finally, bless us with some experiences of joy and excitement. We know you are strength in time of trouble, but you are also a sure foundation upon which to laugh, and sing, and praise, and give thanks. If we are blessed with a smile of pleasure; if we are baptized with healthy laughter; if we are anointed with some kiss of love; give us grace to say so and enjoy it. If we are touched by generous deeds; warmed by affectionate hugs; made at home by acceptance; feel good about a successful project, give us grace to say so and enjoy it. Through Christ. Amen.

46 FIRST PRAYER IN NOVEMBER

O GOD, conductor of the sounds of the universe, your music is all around us if we but have ears to hear. Behold, there is the sound of rain on sidewalk or roof; the melody of a stream as it laughs its way over rough places; the piercing caw of a saucy crow; the gentle tune of a breeze in a pine; the symphonic roar of thunder; the whine of an electric line; the plain song of the mourning dove; the unpredictable melodic abundance of the mocking bird; and the whistle of some happy soul. O God of all creation's music, open our ears that we may be blessed with its beauty.

O God, for music created and shared by our brothers and sisters we give you thanks. For the freedom and exuberance of young voices that give their praise with joyful abandon; for the beauty and skill of the trained and disciplined voice; for the sound of skillful and average voices as they join together in corporate harmony, we give you thanks. For those who practice to assist our praise; for those who share their skill that we may find our spirits lifted into the profound; for all who add to the beauty of our world through the gift of song, we give you thanks.

O God, not all songs are glad songs. Some are sad. Some, tune-filled with memories, will bring tears to our eyes. Some melodic lament will help us cry, and in the crying there is release and healing. Do not spare us the sad songs, for we would be whole persons and life cannot always be joy and praise.

But when we are entrapped, when we are bowed down with pain, when we are confused, when we are angry, when we are disenchanted, empty, depressed, miserable, then, O God, sing us the songs of your compassion. Refresh our memories with the strong, sure chords of your ever present love. Resolve all of our suspension in the full harmony of your purpose. Make us mindful of the pure and simple melody you offer us all in your son, Jesus Christ. And give us grace to learn to hum it, sing it, shout it, live it. In his name we pray, AMEN.

HOW can we sing unto you, O God, when the day is gray and rainy; when the gloomy weather somehow influences our disposition? We can remember yesterday, O God. We can remember that not all days are the same. We can look forward to better days. And even gray days can be lazy days when change of routine allows us the blessing of less things to do and the refreshment of being unhurried.

How can we sing unto you, O God, when the day is filled with pain and disease and uncertainty; when some of us never seem to feel good; when hope itself seems frayed and tattered; when tests and medical knowledge bid us be patient; when the most which can be said is, "We don't know?" We can place our trust in your goodness; place our discouraged souls in your hands; and using the energy and life we have, we can be about some significant task which benefits another. For perhaps if we lose our lives for you or some neighbor's sake we may once again find them; and once again be able to vocalize a song of joy.

How can we sing unto you, O God, when

relationships which are so important are fractured and lying in pieces; when affection has given way to disenchantment; when trust is something which used to be; when comfortable love has turned to bitter disappointment. We can call to mind the love and care we know which is strong. We can pray for ways to renew that which seems tarnished and no longer beautiful. We can refuse to give up while there are still ways to apologize; to work; to rebuild; to forgive. And perhaps love's old sweet song can once again be familiar to us.

How can we sing unto you, O God, when our voices are given full time to other pursuits? How can we sing to you, when we are shouting at stupidity in human affairs? How can we sing to you when we are humming nasty little tidbits over a neighbor's predicament? How can we sing to you when we are preoccupied with counting offenses others have committed against us? How can we sing to you when we forget you are the source and reason for beautiful melody? Forgive us for being still when we should sing. In Christ's name we pray, AMEN.

O LORD GOD, you reveal yourself in the wonders, the mystery, and the order of creation. But the meaning of what we experience; the understanding of the yearnings of our heart; the story of your relationship to humankind; must all come to us by witnesses; those who share by written and spoken word, and who live among us and with us. For all who have contributed to our spiritual pilgrimage and have nurtured our growth in the faith we give you thanks. We remember especially grandparents, teachers, parents, friends who have so faithfully and patiently passed on the promise to us. Our lives are more centered; whole; more meaningful because of their willingness to be witnesses.

Now, lest we forget how we came to know and serve and find our home with you, remind us of our task in witnessing. You know, we are not too pleased by being called to pass on the promise. We don't want to be labeled radical. We often equate being evangelical with having some kind of fever or virus. We don't want to be a nuisance. Faith is a private affair and we certainly don't want to try to force anyone in any direction. And having said all of that, we know, O God, our arguments are hollow. We have a task to do. If we find in our relationship with you, something which blesses us; something which brings meaning to life; something which we lean on in good and bad times, then we are obliged to find some way to invite others into the fellowship which helps celebrate and nurture that blessing. We are not always sure what we should do to pass it on, but make us willing to learn, and gird us for the task. Take away our timidity. Make us bolder in simple offers which invite and include others.

We pause now in prayer for those who have special need. There are those who face physical pain and deterioration; who have bad news about their condition. Be merciful to them in release from pain and despair. Grant them hope and health. If that is not possible grant them peace and courage and wholeness of spirit. There are those who feel distressed, whose circumstances leave them weary with sameness of struggle, who feel power-less to change anything. Bless them with some gift of new life; through Christ. Amen

49 FOURTH PRAYER IN NOVEMBER

O GOD, the messengers and messages of this season overwhelm us. One lures us to travel and get away from it all; another tells us we should give extra time with family and friends. One tells us our hope is in a million to one chance on the lotto; another tells us that we can only prove our love if we get that certain gift that will say it all. Still another tells us that celebration and living it up is the way to break the dull routine of living. Among all the messengers and messages let your Christmas news find its way to our heart, O God, for we need the gifts of joy and peace to bless our lives.

O Lord, our lives know the agony and pain of bad news. We face an operation we didn't expect; we have feelings and emotions that we can't control and experience depression; there are pressures at work which diminish our sense of accomplishment; we find parents unwilling to listen to us—we find children unwilling to communicate with us; we find a friend confused and our friendship seems to be unhelpful. O God, the agony of bad messages is very much a part of our lives. When we are overwhelmed, send some clear and startling message that will penetrate and bring strength and support; some new form of good tidings of great joy.

O God, our lives know the fulfillment of good news. We hear and know that in the gift of the Christ child you gave and give love to the world. We see here a sign of caring; there a demonstration of love. We see here a person lend a helping hand; there an arm of affection and comfort. We see here a look of long standing love; there a smile of encouragement. For all such good news; for all such joy, we give you thanks.

But O God, the mixed messages go on. We hear the message of the world arming for defense or war; we see across the back fence an act of neighborly peace. We read a message of murder and violence; we get a message of the miracle of new birth to a family of friends. We receive a message of misfortune, we hear a message "fear not for I bring good tidings." We experience a message of loneliness; we receive the message, "Lo I am with you." We experience ups and downs and we then hear that "every valley shall be exalted and every hill made low."

O Lord God, in the mixed messages of life, let the Christmas season be a time when we receive good news with such power that for a time; it may be a season of comfort, hope, love, and joy. Amen.

50   FIRST PRAYER IN DECEMBER

HOW can we keep silence this season, O Lord. We are surrounded by a cacophony of sounds which seem to make silence an impossibility. There are the sounds of worried persons who are spending more than they can afford; there are the sounds of impatient persons who wish the slow people would get out of their way; there are the sounds of angry persons who missed a sale item; and there are gaudy commercial sounds intended to put us in the spirit of the season. And we hear it all and are a part of it all. Don't give up on us Lord. We do want to get to the true meaning of this season. If silence will help, then put your hand on our busyness and stay with us until we are willing to listen and ponder something other than that which is earthly.

Keep us, however, from a kind of holy escape. For surely your coming was something deeply earthly minded. Your investment in the world was to come as one of us and one with us. We do not desire to miss the significance of that truth. Whatever we do this season must witness to the connection between you and the world. Show us how to celebrate such good news.

It is a noisy season, O God. so if we must be less than silent, let our voices join those who sing the expectant songs of your coming among us. Let our voices join those who sing the glad melodies of "God with us..." Let our noise be the noise of peace and good will among all person. Let our celebration be a search for simplicity midst complexity; a festival of love midst violence and hate; a time for joy despite the reality of pain and hurt; a time for hope that abides in the face of individual and corporate despair.

We remember those among us who have special need. Those facing dangerous disease; those who must live with unknown futures; those who wish their lives could be less complicated and more simple; those who are afraid to move on because they do not know which direction to go. Be with them to strengthen and support them. And our country, Lord. We are so quick at war and so slow at peace. Encourage all present efforts at helping to further good will on earth. In Jesus name we pray. Amen

L IKE a shepherd, Lord, you feed us. Most of us have
daily bread and to spare. We thank you. But you have
placed us in a community with an increasing unemployment rate. We live where there are hungry persons. Give
them also their daily bread, and give us no peace until we
do what we ought to do in helping to provide and share
our five loaves and two fishes.

Like a shepherd, Lord you feed us. Feed your world
on your bread of life. It is there, but we, like silly sheep,
prefer the junk food of the world's priorities. Teach us, O
God, that the best things, aren't things. Lead us beside
what is truly important.

We know the cup of Christmas always contains more
than happiness. Some of us will miss loved ones; some
will be disappointed by interruptions; some of us will
relive broken hearts; some of us will remember sad time.
Some will be sick and some will face uncertain future.
Be with all who experience disappointment and pain. And
save us from supposingthat the joy of Christmas must be
simon pure, untainted if it is to be real. Allow us to be
blessed in the midst of the way life is. Grant a song, a

smile, a laugh, a surprise, an unexpected hug to grace the feel of Christmas. Let joy come, and make us glad in it.

Like a shepherd, Lord you feed us on peaceful things. You took a towel rather than a sword. This week, wherever leaders of the world meet to talk, let the price of peace be in their conversations. Let them be more concerned for the world's people than for the countdown on their destructive power. Let them be more concerned for quality of life for the future than for who's ahead in carrying the big stick now. O God, not only the lion and the lamb, but let the bear and the eagle abide in peace. Amen.

W E KNOW better, Lord, than to base our Christmas
expectations on who's been naughty and who's been
nice. But if we have expectations of this season which
nag us; which make the season more wearisome than
glad; maybe we should check who's getting our time
priorities. Midst all our plans and purchases, are you
getting a fair share? Are we going more to the mall than
coming to Bethlehem in our mind and memory? Are we
searching for the Christ child in our imagination and our
hope? O God, to season our Christmas celebration with
the spice of joy and meaning, help us to take to heart the
ancient invitation, Venite Adoremus, Dominum; Come let
us adore him, the Lord.

Who puts into the heart the longing for peace? Who
makes us yearn for good will rather than malice? Who
make us dissatisfies and wretches when we harbor
animosity against another? Who makes us angry at
ourselves when our pride promotes brokenness rather than
healing? Venite Adoremus, Dominum. Come, let us
adore him, the Lord.

Who blesses us with simple joy that we take for

granted? Who gives us divine and human love to make life sing? Who gives us the pleasure of laughter, the joy of hugs and kisses, the fun of remembering past good times? Who blesses us with the security of a faith tradition, and who daily gives us the potential for new life, new beginnings, new possibilities? Venite Adoremus, Dominum. Come, let us adore him, the Lord.

Who inspires the real reason for the season? Whose gift began the giving of all good gifts? Who taught us that giving is more blessed than receiving? Who turns us from ourselves to others? Venite Adoremus, Dominum. Come let us adore him, the Lord.

We remember, O Lord, those who find the joy of Christmas hard to bear. A loved one is missed; a tragedy is remembered; an old wound is reopened; an up-to-date uncertainty is accentuated; a continuing brokenness is reaffirmed. For all who find the season more pain than pleasure, grant O Lord that they may in spirit heed the invitation, Venite Adoremus, Dominum; and in coming to you, find rest, and peace for their souls.

O Lord, who renews their commitment to come and adore?

We all do, in the name of Christ our Lord. AMEN.

53 FOURTH PRAYER IN DECEMBER

O LORD, once for us a child was born. He came into a world where people were captive; where injustice was rampant; where some with resources oppressed those who had little. Come again, Lord Jesus.

Once for us a child was born. He came into a world where people counted their arms; where they trusted in the might of their armies; where warfare seemed the only way to settle differences. Come again, Lord Jesus.

Once for us a child was born. He came into a world where people were suffering; where many kinds of sickness threatened life; where pain took its toll without regard to race or station. Come again, Lord Jesus.

Once for us a child was born. He came into a world which had lost direction; which was confused and turned in on itself; which was floundering and thought it was progressing. Come again, Lord Jesus.

Once for us a child was born. He came into a world which needed a sign; which needed a change; which needed Good News. So it is, even with us still. Come again, Lord Jesus. AMEN.

54   FIFTH PRAYER IN DECEMBER
(Christmas Eve)

O LORD, our presence here says something about how special you are to us at this time of year. Our souls long to have the story of your love come down at Christmas relived in our heart. Our spirits wait to hear again your exceptional good news. Whatever our motivation, whatever our reason, whatever our hope, whatever our need, come Lord Jesus. Be born again as our King, our comfort, our joy. Come again as light.

Make it clear to us that your coming is not easy, Lord. Even in this 20th century, you do need the lodging which our willingness to receive you can provide. Break open all our defenses. Announce yourself by any medium. Enter by any means. Refuse to be turned away though we allow no room. Birth within us, again this year, the joy of our salvation.

Lord, even if we are among those who feel a tinge of sadness; even if we are among those whose joy is trained; even if our memories are bittersweet; even if we are lonely in a way we do not desire; O Lord, stir up in us some reasons for joy and happiness. Make our search for you easy as we see a piece of your love in the eyes of a

loved one; as we hear the sound of your voice in a
friendly "a blessed season to you." Bless our ears with
reminders of the wonder of that first heavenly host, in
contemporary sounds of praise; in the infectious laughter
of our children; in the miracle of a baby's cry; and in the
sweet sounds of "hello's." Put the hand of your care on
us in the squeeze of a family member; in the hug of a
friend; in the touch of someone that matters.

Finally Lord, if any among us is part of the reason
for someone's unhappiness; or if unhappiness is someone
else's gift to us; this is the season to make amends. Show
us how to do it. Help us to take initiative to heal
brokenness. And if that is not possible, save us from
allowing someone else's foolishness to control our lives.

O Light of the world, You are the reason for this
season. Be present in what we do and say, Lord, that our
presence throughout this celebration of your coming, may
honor and glorify the wondrous gift given. AMEN.

55 A BENEDICTION

G O NOW!
Go in safety, for you cannot go where God is not.

Go with noble purpose,
and God will honor your dedication.

Go in love, for it alone endures.

Go in peace, for it is the gift of God
to those whose hearts and minds are in Christ Jesus
our Lord. AMEN.

56   A PRAYER FOR GUIDANCE

S HEPHERD Lord, sheep are a part of your wondrous creation. They charm us when they are small,
and bless us year after year with the raw material to
make warm fabric. Yet those of us who have worked
with sheep know how stubborn and stupid they are. They
run from those who want to care for them; who will feed
and give them shelter. Without a worry, sheep will
follow one another into stupid and dangerous places.
Lord, you've made them so they can't be pushed any-
where; they can't be forced to do anything; they can only
be led. Lord, we don't enjoy being likened to sheep, yet
all we like sheep have gone astray. We do turn to our
own way. We need the gentle stay of your staff and the
comfortable guidance of your voice to counsel us.

Shepherd Lord, we go through dangerous places at
our own initiative. Daily we test our freedoms in precarious ways. Eagerly we grasp our wants. Tenaciously we
hold fast to unnecessary and harmful habits. Foolishly we
neglect the healthy care of our bodies and spirits. Com-
pulsively, we feed our anger by nursing bitter memories
and shattered hopes. Lethargically, we muddle along in

the gray routine of life, wondering if this is all there is. O Shepherd of darkened valleys, routinized paths, and pleasant still waters, keep your voice strong and persistent. Be patient with us. Restore our souls and lead us in the paths of righteousness.

Shepherd Lord, we experience shadowed valleys without choosing them. Some of us must live in the specter of physical uncertainty. Some of us must abide in the certainty of pain and increasing debility. Some of us must live with the irreversible anguish of broken relationships. Some of us lose loved ones. Be we old or young, when such valleys come our way, gather us in your arms and hold us in your safety and comfort.

Shepherd Lord, save us from being so concerned about ourselves that we never find the will to risk our lives in causes of justice and neighbor love. It is only in trusting you that we recognize the courage to speak or act bravely. All around us are persons poor in opportunity and resources. There are, near and far, persons who have needs we could help to answer if we took the time to respond. Shepherd Lord, put the crook of your staff on the resources of our life and remind us that inasmuch as we do it to any of these, the least of your children, we also do it to you. AMEN.

57   PRAYER FOR NEW BEGINNINGS

CREATOR God, you initiated the beginning; you continue to care for creation; and you find yet more things to begin. Surely there is a new age coming if we but have the eyes, and the ears and the understanding to behold it. Surely it will emerge if we have the will to invite it and nurture it.

O God of all new beginnings, in the days ahead there will be opportunities to give our energies to the cause of peace. There will be chances to show love of neighbor. There will be occasions to demonstrate kindness and thoughtfulness. There will be chances to work for justice; there will be openings for compassion. The new age is open for the taking. And we do not want to pass, unseeing and unresponsive, any such new opportunities. Save us, O God, from automatic fear of new responses; from anxiety over new requirements. Open us to good changes.

O God of all new beginnings, there is a new day coming. There will be change. And while we know that change is a sign of life, we also know that some change is not welcome. We do not want to lose loved ones. We do not want to have to deal with things like terminal illness. We do not want to be faced with any kind of tragedy. We do not want to leave life before it is finished and we do not want to stay too long and grow infirm and dependent. The life you give us, O God, does not have a "satisfaction" guarantee. It is precarious, and we cannot always control what happens. So some of us will have changes we do not covet. We do pray that when life requires such unwelcome change, you will be close by, to comfort, strengthen, and guide. O God, whatever dismal or painful valley we must traverse, whatever mountain we must cross, it is made more passable by your loving presence.

Oh, but there is a new age coming in which you offer us hope and expectation, O God. We can get ready! New life is a part of your main business. And however that kind of change touches us, it brings a smile and a lift and a song of praise. A new baby will be born which will turn our hearts to joy. A new opportunity will come to excite and challenge. In the midst of old tasks, a new idea will emerge, and our creativity will dance. A nagging old habit will be replaced by a new style of living. And by your spirit and our cooperation, attitudes and addictions which make us prisoner can be set aside and we may taste the freedom for more noble things. In your time, for our sake, let it be so, O God. AMEN.

O THOU Great Host; the one who owns the banquet hall; who sets the table; who prepares the feast; and who issues the invitation to each one of us; there is so little required of us to experience the joy of your welcome table, yet so much in the one thing we must do in order to find our place there. We must choose to be there. We must RSVP with our life. Give us wisdom to make that commitment. Help us to choose life.

Thank you God, that your welcome table is not some smorgasbord in the future, but extends its bounty into this life. By your mercy, we can drink of the healing waters any old day. There is comfort for those who hurt in body and soul; there is wisdom for those who take time to listen and reflect; there is hope for those who are trapped; there is peace for those who are frenzied; there is release for those imprisoned by their anger; there is solace for those disappointed; there are solutions for those who cry out for answers. It is not promised that if we drink of these healing waters we shall never again have to feel pain or disappointment or rough places; only that we will not have to thirst in a life where there is no water to drink. What a welcome table you give us.

Thank you God, that your welcome table provides a place and an occasion for us to celebrate the lilt of life. At your welcome table we may spread abroad our joys: the fulfillment of relationships which bring out the best in us; the support of friends and loved ones; the comfort of those who care; the stimulation of shared treasures; the exhilaration of life tasks which require the best in us. For all such joys freely shared and celebrated at your welcome table, we give you thanks. Good things need to be affirmed, and we do it gladly.

Keep in our minds, O Great Banquet giver, that the feast has other purposes than self gratification. We are commissioned as those who may eat and drink to the full, to live our lives as an encouragement and blessing to the hungry who have mislaid their own invitation. Your request for our presence is not a hidden threat. It is an offer of joy. Teach us how to believe in and communicate the blessing of being at your table rather than the hazard of missing it. For the notice we receive from you is not a subpoena; it is an invitation through which we behold open arms waiting to receive us. Oh, what a welcome table where we may drink healing waters any old day, even today. Thank you God for the invitation. AMEN.

O GOD, you who require so little of us which we
expect you to require, and so much of us which we
are slow to acknowledge; save us from reading our own
character and purposes into your personhood. Speak to
us in word and song that our lives may be in tune with
the true harmony you have in mind for us.

How we long to go forth in peace, O God. But the
world seems to allow for so little peace. There is violence
between countries, and between neighbors and family
members in our own city. and violation of human rights
in our own county. The privileged and underprivileged
lead vastly different lives in a world with abundance for
all. Most of us are richly blessed, yet we fear the time
when we might not be. O God, how can we be of good
courage, hold fast to what is good, and go forth in peace
when we are surrounded by so much which seems to give
us no peace?

Could we, Lord, improve our corporate life; our
family relationships; our sense of meaning and purpose in
life, if we were to make the effort to walk humbly with
you? Is it possible for us, O God, rigid, defensive, protec-
tive, fearful as we are, to get beyond rendering evil for
evil; an eye for an eye; and learn the grace of honoring

all people? Is it possible for us, O God, self centered as we are, to love tenderly and thereby strengthen the fainthearted; support the weak; help the afflicted? Oh Lord, let it be so. If humbly walking with you is strange to us, save us from turning away before we have scarcely begun. If humbly walking with you is a revolutionary experience, save us from the fear of change. If humbly walking with you makes us new creatures, save us from tenaciously holding on to who we've been. Behold the yearning in our heart, O God, the hunger for peace, the longing to go our way rejoicing. Use our symptoms as encouragement to accept your invitation for us to walk humbly with you in your way.

We offer our spiritual energies through you to those who have special needs. In your blessedness, O God, give comfort for the bereaved, encouragement to the discouraged, wisdom to the confused, strength to the weak, health to the sick, love to the unloved. And where we may represent you in any such care, save us from busily or protectively passing by, granting us grace to do enter into their need with your kind of justice and tender love. Through Christ, AMEN.